More Than Words

Dawn Pierce

MORE THAN WORDS

© 2025 Dawn Pierce
All rights reserved.

Paperback ISBN: 978-1-0369-1993-1
Ebook ISBN: 978-1-0369-2305-1

Book design by Sarah E. Holroyd
    (https://sleepingcatbooks.com)

Cover Design by Eccentric Girl Press

Dedications

Saffron, my dear friend and yoga teacher. Thank you for your encouragement and support, which has helped me overcome some tough life challenges. Your lessons is where my love of yoga started.

Cathy, my dear friend and yoga teacher. Your creativity and innovation in teaching yoga, is inspiring and led me to writing this book. Your lessons and yoga retreats will stay with me for a lifetime.

Eleanor, my dear friend. I hope you enjoy reading this book. Whilst finding some comfort and consolation.

Georgie, my beautiful niece. Taken way too soon.

"You're in the arms of an angel now, fly away, fly away."

Mary, my dear friend. Taken way too soon.

"Smile and the world will smile with you."

Contents

The Chakras

You have seven chakras, which are situated along the spine, starting from the base of your spine to the crown of your head. Each of them are associated with a different colour, as shown below.

They are thought to provide energy that helps your organs, mind and intellect work at their best energy.

Practicing meditation, yoga and certain dietary choices, choosing foods that align with the colours of each chakra are believed to balance and harmonize the chakras.

Root Chakra: Associated with grounding, stability and survival.

Sacral Chakra: Linked to creativity, emotions and sexuality.

Solar Plexus Chakra: Related to personal power, confidence, self-esteem and digestion.

Heart Chakra: Associated with love, compassion and connection.

Throat Chakra: Linked to communication, truth and expression.

Third Eye Chakra: Associated with intuition, perception and wisdom.

1

Crown Chakra: Connected to enlightenment, spiritual awareness and connection to the universe.

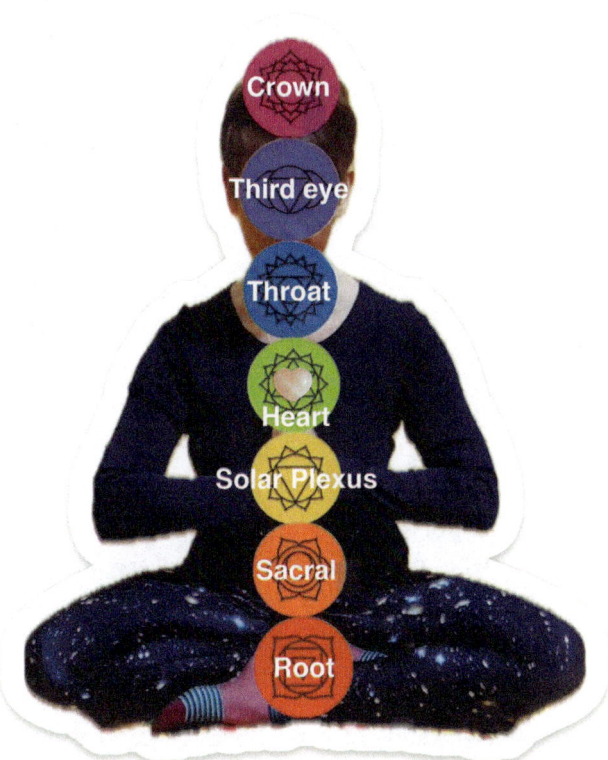

A Soft Whisper from Nature

My yoga journey started many years ago, after researching a form of exercise that would help a chronic lung condition, that I have been living with for most of my adult life.

Yoga as a low impact form of exercise was a great choice for me. Made up of two parts: physical poses, called asana and mindful of breathing techniques, called pranayama. I found both parts beneficial for maintaining my physical and lung health, whilst improving my quality of life.

I also found yoga supported stress management, mental health, mindfulness and improved my quality of sleep.

So, when my yoga teacher organised a yoga retreat, to Dalyan, Turkey, it sounded amazing, so I jumped at the opportunity, not knowing that it would lead me on a magical journey of relaxation, self-discovery, and physical well-being and creativity.

The retreat was located in the most wonderful surroundings, enveloped by magnificent mountains, sweeping lawns and clean air. It was peaceful and quiet; you could hear every sound from Mother Nature. Which brought a sense of calmness, helped me destress, and brought me to a greater sense of appreciation for life.

On the second evening we were asked to take a gift to the yoga studio, that we could share. A gift of love and kindness to oneself that had a ripple effect to others.

In the surroundings of nature, I was inspired to write and share the poem, "A Soft Whisper from Nature." That led to many more poems, writing about my experiences throughout my magical journey.

I am hoping that you, the reader, can also experience and be part of that magical journey through this collection.

The photographs captured on the retreat feature in this book, are amongst a thousand words.

A Soft Whisper from Nature Poem

A soft whisper from nature entered my breath

I swallowed and inhaled it to the deepest of my lungs

Now it rests, deep in my heart and in my mind

It keeps humming a song of love and being kind

The small voice gives me peace and joy

It awakens a sense of the beauty of reality

It encourages me to stop living life based on my needs
for material comforts and greed for oneself

It reminds me that grace and love is a much bigger
need

Dear small whisper of nature, please do not leave me

I cherish you so much

Feel welcome to stay

With that whisper in mind and heart

I shall remember to be kind and spread love, peace
and happiness to all mankind

Beyond The Stars to Infinity

It was a calm, warm and beautiful evening in Dalyan, the skies were clear. It was a perfect evening for star gazing, sailing upon the waters of Dalyan Çayı River.

I could hear laughter from friends boarding the boat like excited children, and just knew we were going to have a fun and special evening.

With everyone settled on board we set sail along the river. Under a fair sky, we laughed, talked, and revealed the warm glow amongst friends.

The sun started to set above the mountains, the colours were amazing all soft shades of red. The sun slowly disappeared, below the horizon, still casting light along the river.

With nightfall upon us the boat gently drifted back with the current and the anchor was slowly released.

The temperature dropped a little so we wrapped up in cosy fleece blankets. The vast expanse of the night sky planets and stars started to appear, I saw Venus, Mars and Sirius, the brightest stars.

After the most wonderful evening of star gazing, when we wished the night could last forever, the boat slowly lifted anchor. We were ready for our journey back to the retreat, the brightness of the night sky was still visible, casting light across the deck. Giving us hope and comfort for a safe journey back along the river.

I saw so many stars, and thought if only I could have one to help guide me through life's trials and tribulations.

Beyond The Stars to Infinity Poem

In the darkness of a mysterious sky

I see a fond magical spark of light, which breaks
through the stillness of the night sky

You light the sky for so many

Guiding us through the path to infinity

You cast magic of our past

Guiding hope for an eternal future

In a world where nearly, everything has a
predetermined end

The thought of something lasting forever is almost
magical

You cast two hundred billion galaxies in front of me

So why can't I just have one?

Just one bright shining star, to guide me through the
journey of life

Your guiding light fills me with love, beauty and
power

Infinity is eternal, something that can't be judged or measured

You leave me with awe and wonder

I hold my breath and wish upon a star

To take me beyond the stars to infinity

Finding that eternal love, beauty and power

While wishing upon on a star

Groves Of Orange

I found inspiration for this poem strolling to the yoga studio. Along a gentle winding path, lined with beautiful groves of orange fruit and blossom trees, surrounded by magnificent mountains.

My body felt warm and relaxed from the early morning ochre sun, and I was focused and ready for the first yoga class of the day.

Orange as a warm colour creates the warmth and security within this poem.

Groves Of Orange Poem

Gentle stroll to the yoga studio through groves of orange blossom

We see beauty of ochre sun within the creation of mother nature

We all join together in movement, nurturing our mind, body and soul

We move from goddess pose, into reverse warrior

Finishing in dancer pose

We awake creative energies

With a new belief in our abilities

Seated in front of a gifted flower, in lotus position

The colour is orange

Like a glowing flame

It gives a feeling of warmth and security

Energising the spleen, the sacral chakra

We feel fresh new blood giving us a clean start

As a well-oiled machine

Leaving the studio

We gently stroll through groves of orange blossom

We see beauty of the ochre sun

Feeling connected with the creation of Mother Nature

Ready to approach the day

With a sense of openness to oneself, others and new experiences of love, peace and joy.

Namaste

I Found Beauty Deep Within My Heart

Inspiration for this poem was found shortly after a yoga class, I was gifted a rose quartz stone in the shape of a heart to represent the heart chakra by my yoga teacher.

The main focus of the yoga class had been connecting and relating to others, healing and filling our life with love and compassion.

I held the heart chakra in my hand, close to my heart, which had been recently bruised, by several loved one's serious cancer and health issues, then my own diagnosis with breast cancer. I could feel my every heartbeat, giving me life, allowing me to invite, healing, empathy, compassion and positivity into my life.

Why not place your hand on your heart? feel every heartbeat, your life's purpose. You are alive for a reason, don't ever give up.

I Found Beauty Deep Within My Heart Poem

I held the gift of the heart chakra in my hand

The energy was real

I felt the love and heat radiating up my arm and deep into my heart

Suspended in one beautifully, eternal moment

I had images of my heart in front of me showing the eternal beauty that I had never seen before

My heart chakra was activated on a physical level

Sending energy to my heart

Along with every heartbeat, pumping fresh blood around my body

Giving oxygen to my lungs

Giving me life

On a spiritual level, opening the heart chakra filled me with love, forgiveness and compassion

With many a setback we found hard to bear

In every heartbeat there is love and true friendship, that help us to care

Enjoy every moment to its fullest. In this way you will
be at peace with yourself

Move ahead and forget your pain, trust yourself you
can start again

The miracle of life

Honour The Heart

We continued to work with the heart chakra, associated with the colour green, it deals with giving and receiving love, with empathy and understanding of others, recognizing that they have their own feelings and values. Showing compassion and kindness, even when they disagree with you or make mistakes.

I am lucky enough to have this with my family and friends, I respect them and in return they respect me.

While the rose quartz is thought to represent self-love, a lifelong journey that we are all on. Treat yourself with kindness and understanding, especially when faced with challenges or setbacks.

Guided Meditation for the Heart Chakra

I would like to invite you, to find yourself a comfortable spot at home, where you won't be disturbed.

Seated on a chair, back straight and feet firmly planted on the ground.

Pay attention to your posture. Back is tall, straight and balanced.

Shoulders are relaxed, allowing you to breathe deeply.

Start by closing your eyes gently and bring attention to your breath.

Take a deep breath in through your nose.

Filling the deepest parts of your lungs.

And slowly exhale through your mouth.

Releasing any tension or stress you may be holding onto.

As you continue to breathe, feel the sensation of the breath entering and leaving your body.

Notice the coolness of the air as you inhale and the warmth as you exhale.

Which will help ground you and keep you in the present moment.

Take time to relax your body.

Pay attention to areas where you're likely to hold some tension.

Allow your forehead and eyebrows to soften.

Feel the muscles in your jaw and face relax.

Now switch your attention to your chest and abdomen.

Notice the gentle rise and fall of your breath.

As you breathe in, imagine that you are breathing in a sense of peace and calm.

Feel your body relaxing, becoming more and more at ease.

Yam is the chant sound for the heart chakra.

Slowly take a deep breath in. Whilst slowly breathing out.

Say the word yam. If repeated, you can feel the vibrations through your throat and chest as you connect with your heart centre.

With every vibration your body will start awakening.

When you are ready, after 30 seconds or longer if you wish, focus on your breath.

Slowly breathing in through your nose and slowly exhale through your mouth.

Which will help you to come back to this present moment.

When you are ready (after thirty seconds, longer if you wish) open your eyes.

Honour The Heart Poem

Seated crossed leg in lotus pose

Holding the gift of the heart chakra

Twelve lotus petals of emerald green sit in the heart centre

The centre of self-love and others, with three below and three above

Where body and spirit become one

Holding the chakra close to my heart, in meditation

Chanting yam

I feel the warmth of emerald green freely flowing

Deep into my heart and lungs

Healing past hurts

Revealing a pure and spiritual place

Feeling love, compassion and forgiveness

With empathy. Opening my heart to a newfound goddess

I receive, offering a heartfelt hug, I hold out a hand

I am here to understand

Namaste

Crowning Glory

As I entered the yoga studio my mind was wandering, I found my place on the mat, facing the magnificent mountains. I sat for a while, looking out at the beautiful vista, quietly listening to the many sounds from nature.

Being mindful, focusing on my breath and senses helped me become more aware of my surroundings.

After a while I found my mind was less cluttered by thoughts, of what might be happening at home. You declutter your home, so why not declutter your mind? By practicing yoga and meditation I clear my mind of negative thoughts, in a safe compassionate environment.

Our yoga Guru welcomed everyone to the class, her voice was calm. Her quiet words carried me off to a calming and spiritual place of my own. Slowly drifting off and relaxing into a deep meditation.

We focused on the crown chakra, located at the crown of the head, in the shape of a lotus flower. A guiding light that shows us the way, and reveals the mysteries within us, finding your true self.

After a while, our yoga Guru, gently guided us out of meditation. It was a beautiful moment of calmness and clarity, I left the yoga studio, feeling calm, peaceful and really happy. It lifted my spirits; my mind was clear and ready to write my next poem.

Guided Meditation

You don't need to be in the surroundings of a beautiful yoga retreat.

Meditation can be practiced anywhere. It gives self-awareness, emotional regulation and relaxation.

I would like to invite you to sit in a comfortable position.

Close your eyes, inhale through your nose. Exhale through your mouth.

With every breath, let all the tension leave your body.

Your face is soft, your shoulders are relaxed, your jaw isn't clenched.

Feel a sense of ease and relaxation spreading throughout your upper body.

Your arms and hands are relaxed whilst gently placed on your lap.

Allow any tension to dissolve.

With your feet placed firmly on the ground, helping you feel grounded.

Continue to breathe slowly and evenly.

Visualize the bright shining light, glowing brightly around your crown chakra.

I'll leave you here for a while, thirty seconds, or for as long as you feel comfortable.

You can feel the calmness in your mind.

With every breath you take.

After thirty seconds, more if you wish.

Slowly start awakening your body.

Gently move your head from side to side.

Bringing movement back to your arms and legs.

Rub your hands together, creating warmth.

Place your hands gently over your eyes.

When you're ready (after thirty seconds, longer if you wish) open your eyes.

Feeling the warmth from your hands.

Crowning Glory Poem

In lotus position, our guru gently guides us into deep
meditation

Eyes closed

We inhale through our noses, exhale through our
mouths

We breathe slowly and evenly

Seeing the petals, white and violet unfurling

Visualise a bright luminous glow of white light

With rays of violet, surrounding my crown

Flowing through my body

The energy around me feels clean and clear

Like the air from the surrounding mountains

With trust, I feel the universe is looking after me

I rise above my earthly worries

Enveloped by the surrounding mountains

Finding inspiration from the gentle whispers of nature

Find calm and wonderment

From awakening to the soothing call for prayer

Sun drenched beaches

Sounds from the sea

Silence of the night

Velvety skies, gazing up at the stars

Drifting off to peaceful sunsets

With new friends

I find harmony of mind, body and soul

With gratitude, compassion and acceptance

We find our true self

Namaste

Ignite Your Inner Fire

For me, igniting my inner fire means embracing my true essence, the energy that lives inside all of us. While I cherish having a great support system of people around me, igniting the inner fire means being able to stand alone, to pursue my passions with confidence and determination.

But to be able to achieve those goals and passions, you need to find balance within your personal life. Remembering that each setback is an opportunity for growth, it's the ability to bounce back from life's challenges, which makes us stronger and even more determined than before.

My main challenge is that there is a fine line between perfection and imperfection, and trying to please everyone. Both of which tend to damper my inner fire, filling me with fear of failure, hindering progress and enthusiasm. Leading to self-criticism, which holds me back from doing the things I'm passionate about. Embracing imperfection and not setting unrealistic goals, helps me grow and evolve along the way.

However, living busy lives, balancing work and family, being unable to switch off the crazy sounds of life, without any time for self-care, can make any of us feel lost and afraid.

Ignite your inner fire is all about caring for the things that are really important to you. Is your flame burning brightly? Or being dimmed by the crazy gusts of life?

Even with lives struggles, my fire usually burns bright, which helps fuel my journey, allowing me to move forward and succeed in things that I'm passionate about. Spending time in nature, finding inspiration for artwork, photography and my new found love for writing.

Guided Meditation

Just as a fire needs tending to grow and thrive, so does our inner flame.

This leads to self-development.

I would like to invite you to find a comfortable place to sit.

Gently place your hands on your lap.

Slowly scan your body and release any tension that you might be holding onto.

Close your eyes,

Inhale through your nose,

Exhale through your mouth.

Visualise the yellow sun.

Feeling the warmth and energy building from your head all the way through your body.

Like a roaring fire, with flames that dance and sway. Strong and powerful.

That ignites the brightest blaze.

The heat and light now fills you.

You feel alive and strong.

Continue to breathe slowly and evenly.

Let the fire guide you forward.

Through confusion and doubt.

It will light your way to discover hidden gifts and a self-strength that you didn't know you had.

Your mind is clear.

Your body is peaceful.

Ready to awaken your inner fire.

When you're ready, (after thirty seconds, longer if you wish) open your eyes.

Ignite Your Inner Fire Poem

Whilst making my way to the yoga studio

Feeling the energy from the sun

Connecting with the splendour of sun-drenched
beaches from earlier in the day

Joining my new friends, firing up our bodies in
mountain pose

Feeling powerful energy

From those magnificent mountains in the distance

A sequence of warrior poses, breath, body and mind

Emotions all intertwined

Slowing my breathing

Body feels stronger

Mind is peaceful

Holding the poses for longer

Feeling the energy of the yellow sun

I feel the energy of fire building in body

Giving me energy

We all become one while chanting ram

The fire within us burns

Blocking all fears, anger and tears

Slow deep breathes from the diaphragm

In through our nose, out through our mouth

Slowly relaxing us into a gentle meditation

Our minds are clear

We have a peaceful body and soul

Leaving the yoga studio

Seeing the yellow sun casting brightness and warmth
   amongst my fellow warriors

Feeling the rising of love, peace and happiness

Deep within my heart

Namaste

Forever Chasing Sunsets

With only a few days left of my yoga retreat I began chasing the sunset, which for me, means trying to see everything I can, before the end of my time away.

I just wanted to embrace every moment of this magical journey. The peace and quiet of the yoga retreat, away from technology, surrounded by nature and breathing in the fresh air. Something beautiful, everything that I had been searching for, a change from everyday life of home.

It made me realise, that life is so precious, and that everyone deserves that period of rest and relaxation.

Forever Chasing Sunsets Poem

On that first evening whilst sailing off for dinner with new friends

Searching for something beautiful

The beginning of a peaceful rest

There is no more beautiful way to end the day, than chasing sunsets

An outlet to sheer beauty

A boundary between day and night

A spiritual and magical time

Sunsets can be glorious and romantic

Peaceful and soul touching

Where the heart meets the soul

I was mindful of time, colour and the beauty of nature

Not wanting the day to end, as for tomorrow to come

Live each day to the fullest

For you don't know what the next day will bring

Live for today

I found myself reaching out

Trying to catch the last rays, upon the haze of the
mountains

The sunset sleeps in the mountains

The mighty mountains

The quiet mountains

The sunset sleeps tonight

And so, must we

The Start of a New Day

Feeling deeply peaceful after starting each day of the yoga retreat quietly. Slowly awakening whilst sipping a morning tea, no talking, no radio, no TV, definitely no scrolling on my phone, unlike home.

I opened my window, taking slow deep breaths, letting the cool morning air enter my body and refresh my lungs after a peaceful night's sleep.

Each morning's yoga session had started with a short meditation, followed by a gentle yoga flow to a soothing rhythm of music. Clearing my mind from negative thoughts, bringing a sense of lightness and ease. Allowing me to focus on the present moment and the positive aspects of life, in a more balanced and hopeful way.

Some of the best things I had found about being on a yoga retreat, were deepening my knowledge and yoga practice in a supportive environment. Eating fresh wholesome food cooked by the most amazing chefs. Enjoying exploring new places and connecting with nature, a refreshing change from everyday life.

Meeting new people who share an interest in yoga and wellness, bringing together a sense of community and connection, creating friendships, that will last a lifetime. Before I am even home, I'm already planning my next yoga retreat!

I felt energised, my senses were awakened. Ready for the start of a new day.

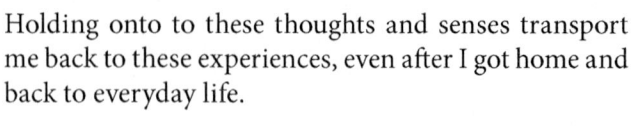

Holding onto to these thoughts and senses transport me back to these experiences, even after I got home and back to everyday life.

The Start of a New Day Poem

Awakening to the soothing call for prayer

Listening whilst mind awakens

To the start of a new day

The window is open with a cooling breeze

In the dawns early light

Seeing the start of a new day

The soft cool wind awakens my senses

See the beautiful vista

Hear the gentle call from nature

Taste the fresh spring water that cleanses my soul

Touch a moment in time

Smell the start of a new day

Entering the yoga studio, finding my place

Seeing our yoga guru in a state of meditation

Slowly awakening

To the start of a new day

My body awakens to the practise of sun salutations

Welcoming the start of a new day

We all become one whilst chanting Om Mani Padmi Hum

"Praise to the jewel in Lotus"

Helping to purify our minds

From negative energies

Feeling the loving calm and positive vibrations

To the start of our new day

A Picture Paints a Thousand Words

The beautiful surroundings of the retreat inspired me to get snapping – I do have such a passion for photography.

I wanted my photographs to tell a story, noticing details, patterns, and textures. Creating peace and calm, making memories through the lens of a camera, making those memories last forever.

When I look back over the pictures I feel the emotions of that moment in time.

And now I get to share the memories with you.

A Picture Paints a Thousand Words Poem

A picture paints a thousand words

It tells a story of a smile, landscape, or a time when things felt perfect

A picture paints a thousand words

Captured in the moment

A picture paints a thousand words that cannot be erased

A picture paints a thousand words of memories that are true

I look at those pictures of a thousand words

Words of happiness

Words of contentment

Words of sheer beauty of sunsets and of stars shining so bright

Memories of times gone by

That are close to my heart

A picture paints a thousand words

Kingfisher

Along with the beautiful vista of the yoga retreat, a river gently flowed alongside the magnificent mountains. Whilst relaxing, appreciating my surroundings, a blue flash of colour appeared, and quickly disappearing deep into the river. I didn't know what this could be, and I held my breath. Until I saw another flash of colour leaving the depth of the river.

To my amazement a beautiful Kingfisher was perched in a tree, what a magnificent sight. I spent many hours watching him busily diving deep into the river, catching fish. The flash of blue moved so quickly, not far from my camera lens.

Once home, I was so disappointed that I hadn't manged to capture the glorious kingfisher on film. This only left me with the determination to find a place, where I could experience that blue flash of colour.

After a little research, I found a local nature reserve where to my delight sightings of kingfishers were documented. With great excitement I planned a trip along with a couple of retreat friends. We packed a lunch, to help us through the long day of kingfisher watching. The nature reserve was beautiful, peaceful and quiet, just like the yoga retreat. We made our way to a bird hide and found a comfortable place to sit.

A couple of hours had passed, we saw many birds, but still no kingfishers. My fellow bird watcher, started to feel the cold and suggested that we should start planning to go home. I convinced her, to wait just a little while longer, the art of bird watching is time and patience.

Then, to my amazement I felt that wonderful moment again. We were overwhelmed with excitement and I managed to capture the kingfisher in all its glory.

Kingfisher Poem

Kingfisher in all your glory, lightning fast over slow
running rivers, you visit to tell your story

Iridescent, showing luminous colours, that seem
to change with every move, flowing from blue
to orange, with some browning of coppery
shades. The scene is the crowning glory of this
marvellously entertaining show

Nesting in burrowed tunnels along river banks,
making small chambers, living on borrowed time,
protecting new life from unwanted predators

Grace and glory of new life, the young have hatched.
Adding to the story of this entertaining show

Fishing for food, slow things down. Quietness is
needed for the spectacular show

Ink black beak, long and sharp, is your weapon for
catching fish. Feeding the young is where you
belong

Sticklebacks, minnows, shrimps and dragonflies are
on the menu. For the nourishment of new life

Hopping out of your burrow onto a firm perch.
Looking down onto the slow flowing water.
Diving to feed the young. Before you drive them
out, ready to start a new life

Every breath holds a moment of stillness. Through the eye of my camera. I'm focused, ready to witness that moment of glory.

My breath holds still. Whilst my eyes adjust to that moment in time. I'm blessed with your beauty one more time. I fail to capture that moment in time

Rainbow of colour I keep in my mind. You were so kind to honour me with the glory of you

The Labyrinth

Labyrinths are used for walking meditation, and this particular one was a single winding circular path, from the outer edge to the centre.

Labyrinths are used world-wide as a way to quieten the mind, calm anxieties, recover balance in life, and enhance creativity. They encourage meditation, which helps reduce stress and gives you an insight for self-reflection.

The slow and mindful journey through the labyrinth can help unwind the mind and help you let go of stress, worries and concerns. I thought it would be a perfect opportunity to gather my thoughts, and think about the stresses, and changes I wanted to make in my life.

I had come to a point in my life where living in London was taking its toll on my physical and mental health. Whilst it offered many opportunities, along with its vibrant culture and endless activities, the fast-paced, high-pressure environment, also led to significant stress. The relentless pace of London living was hard work.

So many hours sat in traffic jams, trying to get from A to B. The constant breathing in of polluted air, which wasn't helping my lung health, was stopping me from doing things, that were important to me.

I needed to be somewhere which allowed me to live a slower pace of life. A place where the air was cleaner, a place where I could have more time, to do things I loved doing.

I realized beneath my intention, was a nagging doubt, I wondered, "How do I do this well enough?" There was my perfectionist tendencies rearing their head again! So instead of trying to make something happen I let the labyrinth help me find my way to self-discovery.

As I walked, I sensed a feeling of wanting to look ahead to the next turn, then the next, until I reached the centre. By the time I arrived, I felt a sense of peace of mind. I could breathe more deeply. It had helped me process the years that were filled with illness. I was ready to leave this behind and look forward to a more relaxed and fulfilled life.

Guided Meditation

I would like to invite you to write down one intention, on a card, this could be desires you wish to focus on and work towards.

Once you have done this, focus on the picture of the labyrinth.

Take a slow breath in through your nose and exhale through your mouth.

Observe the gentle flow of your breath.

Feel the coolness of the air has you breathe in through your nose and the warmth has you exhale through your mouth.

Whilst gently closing your eyes.

Continue with the focus of your breath.

Carry the image of the labyrinth, in your mind.

Within this moment of deep relaxation allow your breath to deepen.

Take a long deep breath in and a long deep breath out.

As you let your breath flow around your body, into any areas, that might be holding onto tension.

Imagine yourself surrounded by nature.

The warm sun is shining down on you.

Helping you relax deeper into relaxation.

As you get used to this new environment and with the written intention in your hand.

Imagine the labyrinth again

And when you're ready, slowly enter one step at a time.

With each step you take lots of memories will surface.

Allow yourself to release what needs to be released.

Into the ground beneath you.

Let the ground in return, offer you exactly what you need.

Continue to focus on your breath, breathing in and breathing out.

As you continue along the path, feeling the ground beneath your feet.

Honouring the moments that have shown up whether they are moments of your past or the journey of your future.

As you look ahead your mind will begin to slow.

Imagine the centre of the labyrinth approaching.

With your intention in mind.

Slowly make your way to the centre.

Just take a while to think about your intention.

Do you need to leave it behind?

Or do you feel ready to embrace that intention?

It's your choice.

After a while, (thirty seconds, longer if you wish) focus on your breath again.

When you feel ready, slowly make your journey out of the labyrinth.

One step at a time.

Walking the labyrinth can trigger lots of emotions.

If at any time you feel worried.

Please feel free to stop.

And calm your mind.

The labyrinth will help you find your way.

The Labyrinth Poem

Starting the journey is often paused with thoughts of
   failure, self – doubt

Paused – trying to find the cause

Mindfulness takes a step back

Setting a big goal

Just keeps adding to lives stack

It's not about the goal

Big goals are scary

Mind is drowsy

The goal Is not something that we can start today

The journey is something that we can start today

Mindfully, one by one, we enter the labyrinth

A journey to our own centre

A moment to remember

With that goal becoming a journey

A journey to your inner soul

The labyrinth will help you find your way

Through turns, my mind is quiet

No longer turning in circles

My heart is opening

My body is grounded

I have that hunger to follow it through to the centre

I slow down and take a break

From those everchanging paths through life

I embrace the gentle turning, releasing everything

In meditation I reach the centre

I received creativity, love and peace

Standing still, head bowed

I prepare myself for the journey out

With mind, body and soul connected

Feeling calm and contented, with the gifts I received

I slowly make my way out of the labyrinth

Out of the labyrinth

I received that journey without any goals

A journey of creativity

Love and peace

One step at a time around the labyrinth

It's your journey to inner peace

Release, receive, embrace the new gifts

Without any goals

With a start to a new journey

Namaste

Mountain Top Tree

I'm a botanical artist, a type of art that is both artistic and scientific, and means that I study all different types of plants.

So, the retreat was in the perfect environment to take note of all the flora on offer. I found such pure inspiration whilst gazing up at all the trees on the top of the mountains, it was a botanical artist's dream come true!

Staying with the beautiful view, finding peace of mind, our yoga guru guided us in to a gentle meditation.

Feeling refreshed with a new sense of creativity, I was inspired to write my next poem.

Guided Meditation

The focus was on the root chakra, situated at the base of our spine, the colour is red.

When we hear the word "root" you might picture a plant, with a sturdy stalk, which tethers it to the earth below.

The root chakra is the driving force that gives us the energy to live our daily lives.

Close your eyes.

Breathe slowly and evenly, in through your nose,

Out through your mouth.

Visualise a glowing red light at the base of your spine, radiating warmth and energy.

Visualise the trunk of your favourite tree.

Growing down from the base of your spine.

Rooting deep into the earth below you.

Whilst slowly breathing out.

Release all negative thoughts.

Sending them down the tree trunk.

Deep into the earth.

You are grounded and connected to the earth.

You are safe and secure in your body.

Feel the warmth of the red light grow stronger with each breath.

Anchoring you firmly to the earth.

Imagine roots from your body.

Rooting deep into the earth below you.

Feeling safe and secure from the warmth of the red glowing light.

All your cares simply melt away.

Deep down into the earth.

Focus on your breath again. When you're ready, (after thirty seconds, longer if you wish) open your eyes.

Mountain Top Tree Poem

Far away in the distance

Trees have been growing for thousands of years

Upon the mountains casting fountains of heavenly
    hues

Wanders and dazzles of where they dwell

Roots growing out and down into the mountain

Bringing up nourishment from the earth

Giving the tree what it needs to be healthy

Grow stronger and flourish for thousands of years

Whilst gazing out at the trees on top of the mountains

A sunset appears, the colour is beautiful

Soft shades of red

Taking care of the root chakra

Giving a strong foundation to life

Like a tree growing roots

Deep into the mountain

No matter what the wind blows my way

My roots will be strong and deep

Now in savasana slowly entering a feeling of deep relaxation

Feeling support from the earth beneath me

All my cares and worries simply melt deep down into the earth

The mountain top tree gave me nourishment to be healthy

Grow stronger, and flourish with creativity

Namaste

Time Gone By

After a relaxing yoga class and wholesome breakfast, my mind was calm and focused on the afternoon adventures.

I boarded the boat with friends, ready for a magical journey. Everyone settled down, eagerly waiting for the adventure to begin.

The captain lifted anchor, and we set sale on fair waters, embarking on a special boat ride to discover hidden mysteries. I didn't want to miss anything, so kept my camera to hand, patiently waiting to capture a moment in time.

I found something quite magical about being on a boat in the ocean. I felt the warm breeze on my face. My body gently swaying from side to side, along with the water curling off the bow. I loved the feeling of being one with the boat and nature.

The coastal area of Dalyan was one of the most beautiful areas that I had ever seen. There are many coves and sheltered bays, I spotted a variety of birdlife and Sealife, purple herons, great egrets, black winged stilts, loggerhead turtles, bass, mullet, and seabream.

The captain wasn't in a big hurry to go anywhere, I truly felt I was on holiday, so was happy with the opportunity to relax. Everyone was starting to feel hungry, we anchored boat, fresh fish were caught and a wholesome lunch was lovingly prepared.

After a relaxing lunch, I enjoyed a swim in the deep crystal-clear waters. Gently floating on my back, I enjoyed the warmth of the sun on my face.

Back on board anchor was slowly lifted ready to sail towards the Çayı River. On the approach our boat sailed through lush green mangrove trees. The boat glided silently, causing ripples, as we ventured deeper into the heart of the Çayı River.

I felt my body relaxing as the boat gently swayed from side to side, almost drifting into a deep meditation, but not wanting to miss anything, I gently brought myself back to the moment in time.

As we sailed deeper along the river, we anchored in a sheltered cove. The moon rose and the water was a mass of sparkling diamonds, from the mystical carved tombstones, along the cliff face. it was such a magical sight. I felt so lucky to have been able to be part of this magical journey, memories made, that would last a lifetime.

Time Gone by Poem

Letting my eyes follow the beautiful scenery on board

Sailing upon the waters of Dalyan Çayı River

My eyes drift up to what appears to be ornate cliff
dwellings

Dwellings of a once forgotten society

Wondering what might be inside those mighty
dwellings

My eyes look deeper

Seeing carvings on the sheer rock walls

Empty, with no signs of life

Within those mighty dwellings of times gone by

In a time gone by

On top of the mountains

Watching the river below

Reaching the souls of the living

Seeing the new society

Prosper and grow

The Power Of Unity

Each day my yoga friends and I came together with a common purpose and discovered more that we had in common. The very essence of yoga which means 'union' where we can open our hearts and work on accepting every part of ourselves.

Within the developing community, we slowly started to share our struggles.

Each evening, we would meet in a quiet place for Sangha, a group of like-minded individuals who gather to support each other, through the power of speech. With awareness, understanding, acceptance, harmony and love within the developed community.

The heart of Sangha is learning to listen to others without interrupting. A precious stone was passed around the group, the person left holding the stone had the opportunity to talk.

Listening was not just about hearing words – it was about understanding and being present. We often speak to be listened to, but being heard and understood is only sometimes guaranteed.

We may be pouring our hearts out, or sharing inspirational ideas, only to realize that the other person isn't fully present, or they might interrupt you mid-sentence.

Sangha taught me and the community, to be mindful

of what we were hearing and not jump in before the end of another person's speech. Being mindful can enhance your understanding. Helping you have a stronger connection with others.

The Power of Unity Poem

Feeling relaxed and energised

After a day of sailing out to mysterious coves

Cleansed from the deep blue waters

Quiet and peaceful memories spent with friends

We find our places in the yoga studio

Welcoming the magnificent mountains

Gentle whispers from nature

Clearing our minds

We join together in unity

With perfect harmony, between mind and body

Our guru guides us through gentle poses

To awaken the throat chakra

Slowly drifting into mediation

I see the colour blue

Inhaling deeply, exhaling slowly

My body is still

My mind is peaceful

Free form negative thoughts

Our guru slowly guides us back

To a moment in time

Our voices become one, whilst chanting hum

Sharing a wholesome dinner

Our bodies feel cleansed

With a feeling of freedom and empowerment

We join together in a sacred place for Sangha

Back to the present moment

We touch on positivity

We touch on our own truths

With a new found confidence

We share our thoughts through speech

Without judgement

We don't need to be like others

Just be yourself

No need to have perfect health

No need to have a perfect mind, without anxiety of worries

With the power of unity

We can listen and understand

Creating more peace and joy

Giving nourishment to you, others and Sangha

Namaste

Enjoy The Silence

Being away from technology and everyday life gave me the opportunity to tap back into my inner child

I loved the silence of the yoga retreat, it encouraged mindfulness, allowing me to fully engage with my surroundings and experiences. A sense of nurturing a deeper connection with myself and helped me clear my mind, and increased my creativity.

With each day of the retreat I found my inner child becoming healthier, I spent time doing things that I truly enjoyed. Was more playful than usual and laughed so much, practiced meditation and creative visualisation, which helped me find inspiration for more writing.

Finding my inner child was a beautiful reminder that joy and light-heartedness are essential. These moments of fun and connection can be a source of comfort and self-development, especially when facing life's challenges. Living with a chronic lung condition and a previous diagnosis of breast cancer had understandably sometimes held me back from those fun moments, that I experienced on the yoga retreat.

Enjoy The Silence Poem

In the peace of the night

Under velvety purple skies

Drifting into the silence of the night

In the silence of the night

The world is in slumber

My mind races intertwined

With thousands of thoughts

Closing the door to the day

Slowly join the world in slumber

Silence of the night where dreams are made

Chasing my dreams into the sky without any limits

Where the world seems so magical

In my dreams

I escape from everyday life

A place where I can find my inner child

Deep in the forest

Fairies and unicorns sit under magical trees

Slowly awakening to the soothing call to prayer

I open the door to the start of a new day

Entering the silence of the yoga studio

I find my place

Waiting for our yoga guru to take us through a gentle
flow of poses

To awaken the third eye chakra

Visualise a strong white light

Glowing from the space between the eyebrows

Whilst flowing from downward dog into eagle pose

Closing my eyes

Bringing awareness to the third eye space

Finishing in child's pose

As all the negative energy leaves my body

I feel grounded and secure

We all become one whilst chanting OM

Deepening our spiritual connection

With wisdom and knowledge

Our guru offers a hand of gemstones

I chose purple sapphire

Now an angel card offering

I chose enchantment

Sat in easy pose

Head bowed

I drift into meditation and visualise with clarity

Deep in the forest

Where fairies and unicorns sit under magical trees

Breathe deep

Dive deep into your inner child

Where dreams do come true

The Ocean Whispers

Dalyan has the most wonderful beach, and vast and expanse of water, just seemed to last forever, a place, where I could escape. The sight, smell, sound and touch of the ocean were enough to make me feel at peace and relaxed, it's a place full of wonders that will never fail to amaze me.

Whether I stepped into the sea to swim, or connected to the ocean in my mind. The water offered me an opportunity to cleanse, my mind, body and soul.

The ocean holds another world, of untold mysteries. I loved just sitting on the warm sand, with the ocean in front of me. The colour was deep blue, it made me feel so calm. Listening to the waves, gently rolling onto the sand beneath me. Gently swayed me into a calming meditation.

Guided Meditation

If you're far away from the sea that's ok, I can take you there.

I would like to invite you to close your eyes.

Whilst feeling the gentle sea breeze on your face.

Breathe in through your nose and exhale through your mouth.

With every breath.

Simply imagine the rhythmic whooshing of waves.

Like a beautiful melody.

Rising from the depth of the ocean floor.

At times, your mind might wander.

When it does, gently bring your focus back to your breath.

Hearing the rise and fall of the ocean waves, with every breath you take.

Allow yourself to be mesmerized by the ocean waves.

Rising and falling.

Breathing in harmony with the ocean.

In and out.

Embracing the experience.

Breaths becoming slower and easier.

Calming your mind and body.

Releasing tension.

Like the mighty ocean releases the water.

Allowing the waves to relax and return to gentle calm.

When you're ready, (thirty seconds or longer if you wish).

Open your eyes.

The Ocean Whispers Poem

Ocean whispers that take you to a mediative state

Feeling that inner calm

With a deep peace within

Loving the magical feeling of being barefoot on the
beach

With the sand between your toes

Standing ankle deep in the ocean

Which stops you for a moment

Feeling the waves lightly washing over your feet

As the water washes back out to sea

Feeling your feet sink into the sand

Which makes you feel so grounded and connected
again

Close your eyes for a moment

Feeling the gentle breeze on your face

You hear the waves whispering a soft slumber song

On the shadowy sand

Sea foam against the shore

Casting patterns of secret tales of life not seen

The ocean whispers peace, joy and happiness

A place where you can escape

In mind body and soul

Find that deep inner peace

Sharing That Moment in Time

In our fast-paced world, where I often overlook the importance of living in the moment, cherished memories are incredibly valuable.

The yoga retreat was a journey through life itself, more than just visiting a place on holiday, I discovered a lot about myself. Delving into the emotional, spiritual and intellectual aspects of my life.

Through my journey on yoga retreats, I've realised that the most valuable things in life aren't material possessions, but the memories and happiness you create.

As I look back on my journey, I can see how the retreat has changed my perspective towards life, enjoying the simple things and the importance of making lasting memories. Helping me to understand different cultures and connecting with people, and to see the world differently.

Memories made are now memories to share with you.

Sharing That Moment in Time Poem

Moments that allowed us to feel the light-heartedness of life

Moments of where our spirits were let free

We made so many heart-warming memories of times

When we had fun together

Whilst sharing a journey of magical moments

We shared that gentle whisper from nature

In a space where we let our inspiration for nature speak

We shared the beauty, magic and wisdom of those magnificent mountains

We shared the power of energy through the moments of Sun salutation

A continuous flowing sequence

Our bodies awakened to the honourable rising of the sun

We shared the calming sounds of chanting

Om Mani Padme Hum

Our voices came together

Along with the healing of mind, body and soul

We shared those moments of quietness

Reflecting and sharing our thoughts

Mixed emotions of great peace, joy and happiness

We shared Sun drenched beaches

While welcoming soulful sunsets

Brightness of stars guiding us through to the end of
    another magical day

Memories made with friends

Memoires of happiness, joy, love and peace

Memories made are now memories to share

Namaste

Take Me Back Poem

Home from a magical journey

Take me back to that place

Away from the demands of everyday life

Take me back to that place

Where the mind could be free from any cares

A place where I felt safe

To accomplish things

I never thought was possible

Take me back to the place

Where I could breathe in the clean air

Which didn't pollute my lungs with every breath

Take me back to the sweeping lawns

Landscaped vistas

Take me back to the ocean

So wide to drift into silence

Take me back to the sunsets

Bright, soft shades of orange

Take me back to those friends

Take me back to that overwhelming belonging

Take me back to where I belong

I Return Poem

Returning home with thoughts

From that sacred place

That gave me space

Space to connect with one's inner soul

And nurture that joy of mother nature

Deep thoughts of joy and peace

Gazing up at the stars

Whilst wrapped in a fleece

Gentle sways of the ocean so wide

Prayers of peace upon the tied

Great joys of serene beauty

Capture the scene of sunsets

That cast such calming colours

Closing eyes and hearing laughter

My heart flutters along with happiness

Finding love, peace and happiness at that sacred place

Slow paced with warm memories

One day I shall return to that sacred place

But for now

I will treasure those moments

Of great peace and joy

I Miss Poem

Slowly awakening to the soothing call for prayer

Chanting to people across great distances

The morning silence

Whilst making my way to the yoga studio

Through flora lined paths

Enveloped by the surrounding mountains

The feeling of warmth and love

whilst we sit in silence

Waiting for our guru to emerge from her moments in
meditation

The gentle morning awakening of mind body and soul

Those slow morning breakfasts

Giving nourishment for the day

Those gentle whispers of nature

From the surrounding mountains

The magical moments

Sun-soaked beaches

The sounds from the ocean Gazing up at the stars

Whilst drifting off to peaceful sunsets

Feeling blessed to have been part of such an amazing
journey

With such beautiful companionship from new friends

Hold close to the heart those memories

Of great peace and joy

Farewell Story

On my return from my yoga retreat and back to every-day life. I knew that the lessons I had learned whilst on the retreat would stay with me long after the trip had ended.

The retreat had given me more than just a break from daily routine. It had provided a space for deep reflection, healing and growth.

A space that I needed to find space and time to reflect on my experiences, how I felt emotionally, how I felt in my body, and what I had experienced in myself. As well as what I wanted to carry forward in my life.

Practicing yoga twice a day, gave me much more than energy and a brighter mood. It increased my mental and physical energy and enthusiasm to do things, that I truly enjoy doing.

I loved the time spent doing yoga surrounded by nature, in return it gave me a greater love of creativity and the natural world. This is where my writing journey (and this book) began.

I think the biggest thing I brought home with me, was the importance of self-care and mindfulness. In my everyday life, it had been so easy to lose sight of what truly mattered. I left the retreat, not only feeling relaxed and refreshed, but with a greater sense of the changes I needed to make in my life.

The biggest being a move to the coast, it has given me the space and time I needed, away from the hustle and bustle of London life, allowing me to follow the things I'm truly passionate about.

The air is fresher, I'm surrounded by nature, and I get to see the ocean every day. Living by the coast is a paradise of mindfulness and beauty. I have a full heart and a peaceful mind.

It's time to say farewell, to you, my reader.

I hope you have enjoyed my magical journey to self-discovery.

Your Thoughts and Personal Reflection

About the Author

Dawn was born and educated in West Yorkshire and moved to London for a career working in the care profession. Unfortunately due to a chronic lung condition, she was forced to give up working with sick children – a job she loved. Dawn was determined to do something with her life and started to pursue her love of creation within the natural world, along with yoga. After going through intensive treatment for breast cancer, she once again turned to creation within the natural world through botanical art, photography, along with yoga and nature inspired poetry.

Dawn recently moved with her husband and dogs to a small coastal town, and has found that this, along with her artwork, photography and poetry has helped her create a safe place to escape her health issues.

Printed in Dunstable, United Kingdom